GRADE
1

Spanish

Published by Brighter Child®
an imprint of Carson-Dellosa Publishing LLC
Greensboro, NC

D0128674

Pronunciation Key

Use the pronunciation key below to learn how to say and make the sound of each Spanish letter.

Spanish Letter	English Pronunciation of Letter	The Sound the Letter Makes	Example of the Letter Sound
a	ah	ah	pot
b	be	b	bat
c	say	k or s	cat, city
d	de	d	dog
e	eh	e	pet
f	efe	f, ph	foot
g	hey	g, h	go, hand
h	ache	silent	silent
i	ee	ee	feet
j	hota	h	hot
k	ka	k	cake
l	ele	l	lemon
m	eme	m	mind
n	ene	n	no
ñ	eñe	ñ	onion
o	o	o	boat
p	pe	p	pot
q	ku	ku	cool
r	ere	r	robe
s	ese	s	so
t	te	t	toe
u	oo	oo	pool
v	ve	v	vine
w	doblay-oo	w	we
x	equis	ks	exit
y	ee griega	y	yellow
z	seta	s	suit

Note: The letters "t" and "d" are pronounced with the tongue slightly between the teeth and not behind the teeth.

Brighter Child®
An imprint of Carson-Dellosa Publishing LLC
P.O. Box 35665
Greensboro, NC 27425 USA

Printed in the USA • All rights reserved.   ISBN 978-0-7696-7631-9

08-056137784

Table of Contents

Numbers

Say each number out loud in English and then in Spanish.

uno

dos

tres

cuatro

cinco

4

Numbers

Say each number out loud in English and then in Spanish.

5

Numbers 1–5

Say each word out loud.

uno		1
dos	 	2
tres	  	3
cuatro	   	4
cinco	    	5

Numbers Review

Write the number next to the Spanish word. Circle the correct number of animals for each number shown. Then, color the pictures.

uno

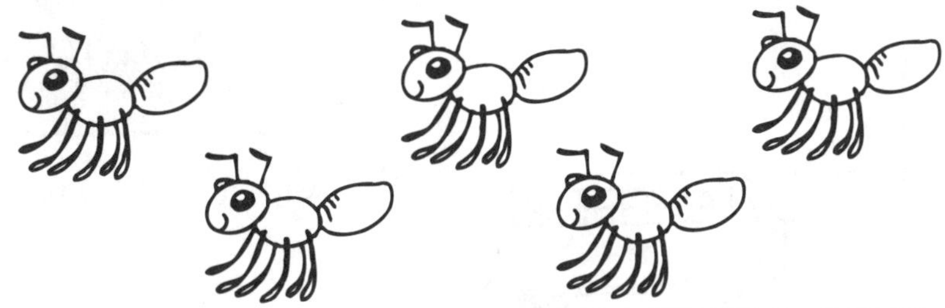

cinco

dos

cuatro

tres

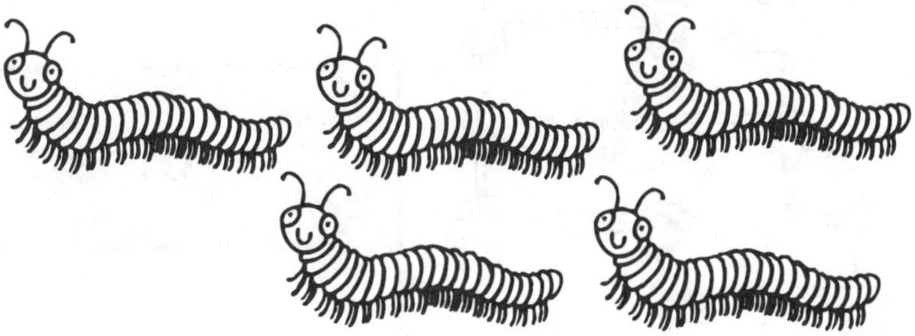

Matching Numbers

Draw a line from the word to the correct picture. Then, color the pictures.

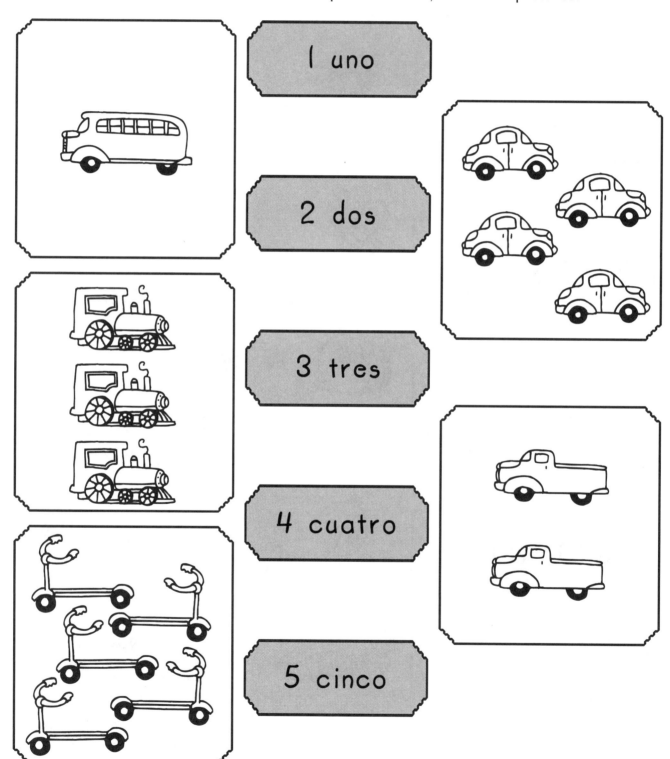

1 uno

2 dos

3 tres

4 cuatro

5 cinco

8

Number the Stars

Draw the correct number of stars next to each number.

uno

dos

tres

cuatro

cinco

1–10 Matching

Draw a line to match each object to the number that is written in Spanish.

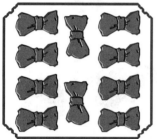

uno	1
dos	2
tres	3
cuatro	4
cinco	5
seis	6
siete	7
ocho	8
nueve	9
diez	10

Count the Cookies

In each box at the left, write the number that matches the Spanish word. Cross out the correct number of cookies to show the number written in Spanish. The first one is done for you.

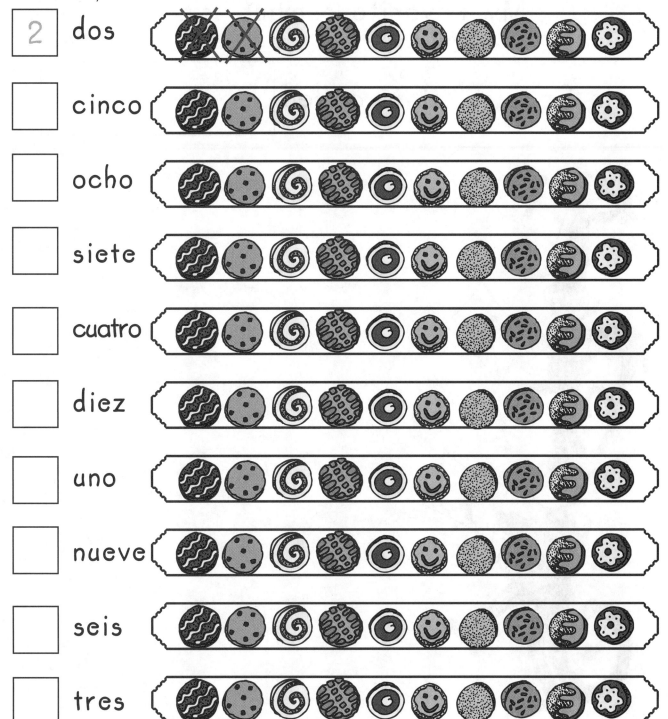

2	dos
	cinco
	ocho
	siete
	cuatro
	diez
	uno
	nueve
	seis
	tres

11 Spanish: Grade 1

My Favorite Number

Write your favorite number from 1 to 10 in the boxes. Draw a picture to show that number.

My favorite number is ▢ .

In Spanish, it is called ▭ .

12

Circles 1–10

Draw the correct number of circles in each box.

uno		seis	
dos		siete	
tres		ocho	
cuatro		nueve	
cinco		diez	

Coloring 0–10

Color or circle the number of butterflies that shows the number written in Spanish.

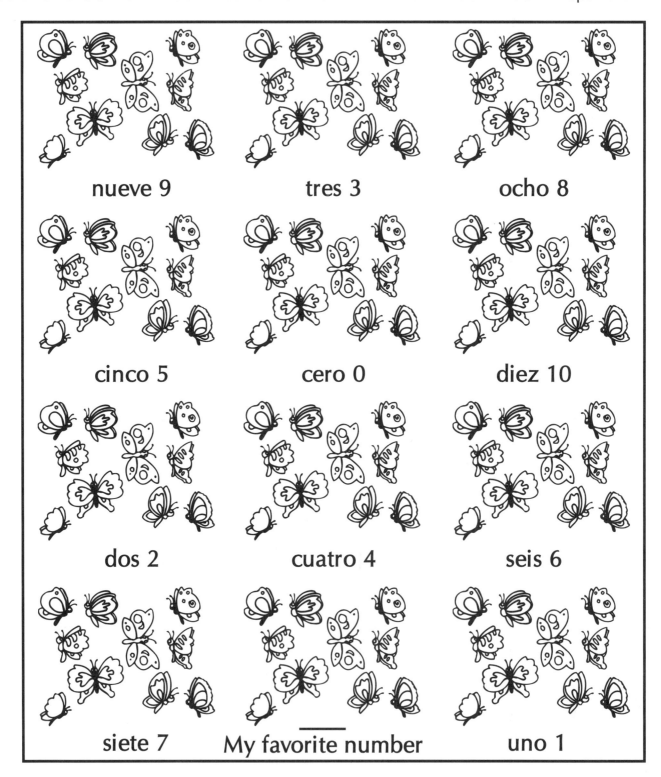

nueve 9   tres 3   ocho 8

cinco 5   cero 0   diez 10

dos 2   cuatro 4   seis 6

siete 7   ____ My favorite number   uno 1

Spanish Alphabet

Say the Spanish alphabet out loud. Find the letter that does not appear in the English alphabet.

EL ABECEDARIO (EL ALFABETO) EN ESPAÑOL

Aa	a	Jj	jota	Rr	ere
Bb	be	Kk	ka	Ss	ese
Cc	ce	Ll	ele	Tt	te
Dd	de	Mm	eme	Uu	u
Ee	e	Nn	ene	Vv	ve
Ff	efe	Ññ	eñe	Ww	doble ve
Gg	ge	Oo	o	Xx	equis
Hh	hache	Pp	pe	Yy	i griega
Ii	i	Qq	cu	Zz	zeta

Rhyming Vowel Practice

Say these sentences out loud:

A, E, I, O U, ¡Más sabe el burro que tú!

A, E, I, O, U, ¿Cuántos años tienes tú?

Listening Practice

Say the Spanish word for each number out loud.
Write the first letter of the words you hear.

1 _____   4 _____   7 _____

2 _____   5 _____   8 _____

3 _____   6 _____   9 _____

Color the letters of the Spanish alphabet. Say them in Spanish as you color them.

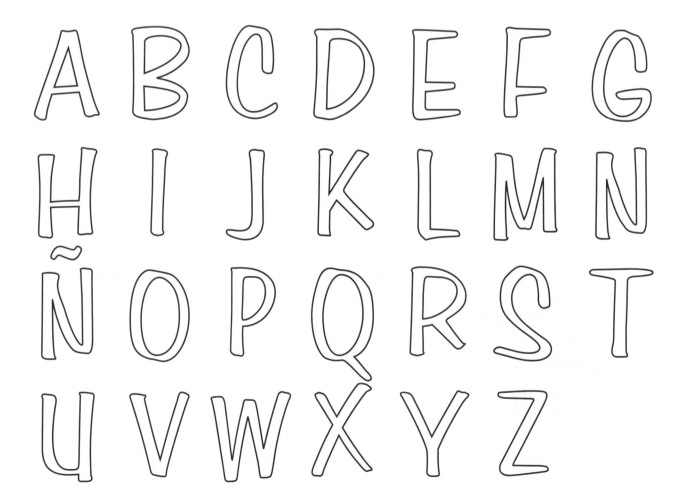

Parts of Speech

Say the word out loud in English and then in Spanish.

you (informal)

tú

you (formal)

usted

pretty

bonita

ugly

feo

Parts of Speech

Say the word out loud in English and then in Spanish.

happy

alegre

sad

triste

to read

leer

to play

jugar

to eat

comer

Introductions and Greetings

Look at each picture. Guess what each person is saying. Then, say the phrase out loud in Spanish.

¡Hola!

?

Juan

¿Cómo te llamas?

Me llamo...

19

Introductions and Greetings

Look at each picture. Guess what each person is saying. Then, say the phrase out loud in Spanish.

¿Cómo estás?

bien

así, así

¡Adiós!

mal

Introductions and Greetings

Say the Spanish introductions and greetings out loud.

¡Hola!		Hello
¿Cómo te llamas?		What is your name?
Me llamo...		My name is...
¿Cómo estás?..		How are you?

bien	mal	así, así

¡Adiós!		Good-bye

Pictures of Greetings

Say the greeting out loud. Circle the picture that tells the meaning of each word.

¡Hola!		
¿Cómo te llamas?		
Me llamo...		
¿Cómo estás?		
bien		
mal		
así, así		
¡Adiós!		

Days

Say the days of the week out loud in English and then in Spanish.

lunes   miércoles   viernes   domingo

martes   jueves   sábado

Monday	Tuesday	Wednesday	Thursday	Friday	Saturday	Sunday
		1	2	3	4	5
6	7	8	9	10	11	12
13	14	15	16	17	18	19
20	21	22	23	24	25	26
27	28	29	30			

23

Spanish: Grade 1

Months

Say the months of the year out loud in English and then in Spanish.

enero	febrero	marzo
abril	mayo	junio
julio	agosto	septiembre
octubre	noviembre	diciembre

24

Seven Days

Copy the Spanish words for the days of the week. In Spanish-speaking countries, *lunes* is the first day of the week.

Monday	**lunes**	_____
Tuesday	**martes**	_____
Wednesday	**miércoles**	_____
Thursday	**jueves**	_____
Friday	**viernes**	_____
Saturday	**sábado**	_____
Sunday	**domingo**	_____

Draw a line to match the Spanish and English days of the week.

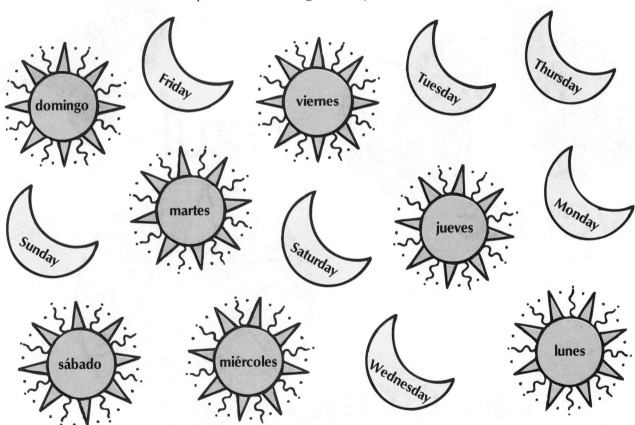

Name _____

Colors

Say the color of the picture out loud in English and then in Spanish.

negro

blanco

verde

azul

amarillo

Colors

Say the color of the picture out loud in English and then in Spanish.

café

anaranjado

morado

rojo

rosado

Colors Introduction

Say the words out loud. Color the word with the correct color.

28

Food

Say the name of the food out loud in English and then in Spanish.

leche

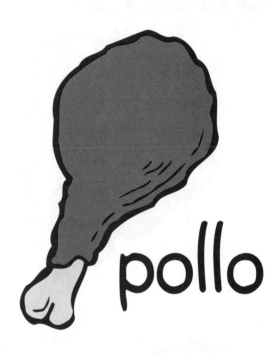

pollo

ensalada

Food

Say the name of the food out loud in English and then in Spanish.

queso

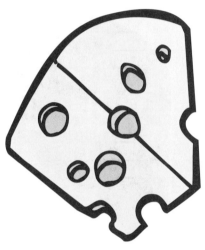

papa

pan

jugo

30

Food and Drink

Say the Spanish words for some delicious foods and drinks out loud.

queso		cheese
leche		milk
papa		potato
jugo		juice
pan		bread
pollo		chicken
ensalada		salad

Spanish: Grade 1

My Meal

Draw or cut out pictures of food and glue them on the plate to make a meal. Which food is your favorite?

Mi comida

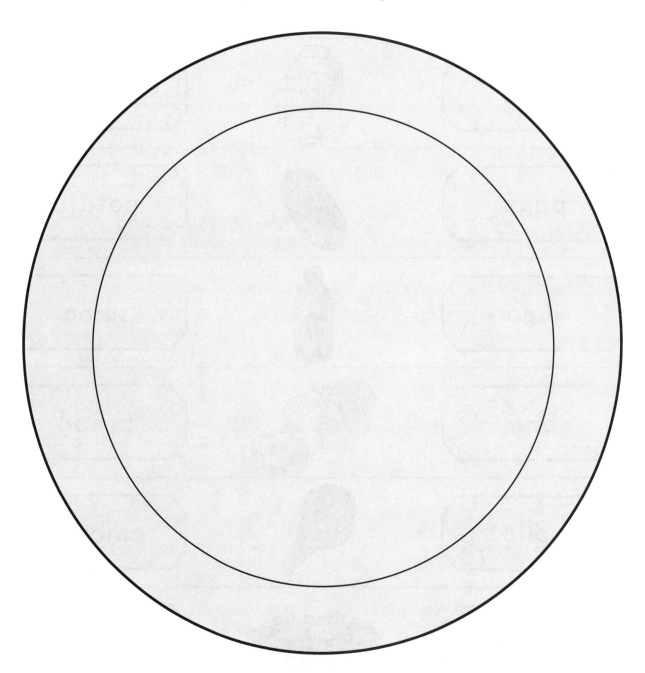

32

Animals

Say the name of the animal out loud in English and then in Spanish.

perro

pájaro

rana

pez

vaca

Spanish: Grade 1

Animals

Say the name of the animal out loud in English and then in Spanish.

abeja

pato

gato

oso

caballo

34

Animal Crossword

Use the picture clues to complete the puzzle. Choose from the Spanish words at the bottom of the page. One is done for you.

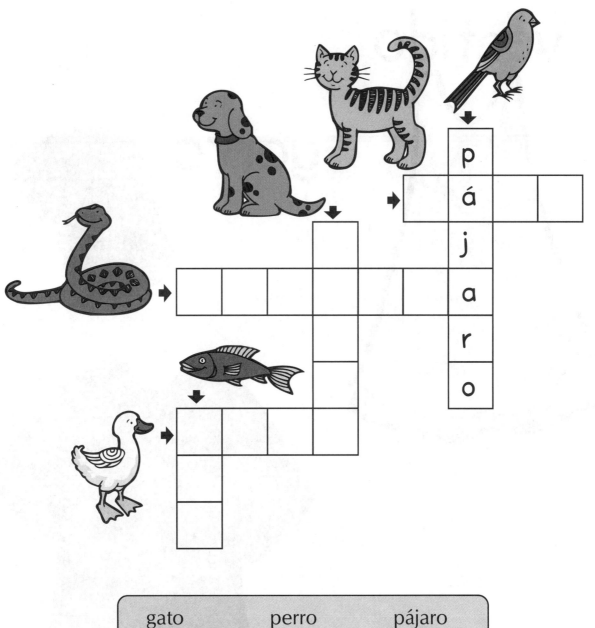

| gato | perro | pájaro |
| pez | pato | culebra |

Spanish: Grade 1

Clothing

Say the name of the article of clothing out loud in English and then in Spanish.

vestido

gorro

camisa

36

Clothing

Say the name of the article of clothing out loud in English and then in Spanish.

calcetines

zapatos

pantalones

Clothing

Say each word out loud.

| camisa |  | shirt |

| pantalones |  | pants |

| vestido |  | dress |

| calcetines |  | socks |

| zapatos |  | shoes |

| gorro | | cap |

Clothing Match-Ups

Draw a line from the word to the correct picture. Color the picture.

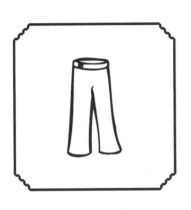

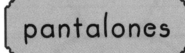
camisa

pantalones

zapatos

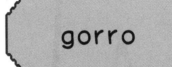
gorro

vestido

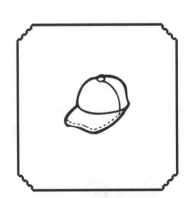

calcetines

How Are You?

Draw or cut out pictures of clothes to make a boy or girl. Write the names of the clothes next to them in Spanish.

40

The Face

Say the name of the body part out loud in English and then in Spanish.

The Face

Say the name of the body part out loud in English and then in Spanish.

cara

boca

pelo

42

What's on Your Face?

Say each word out loud. Copy each word.

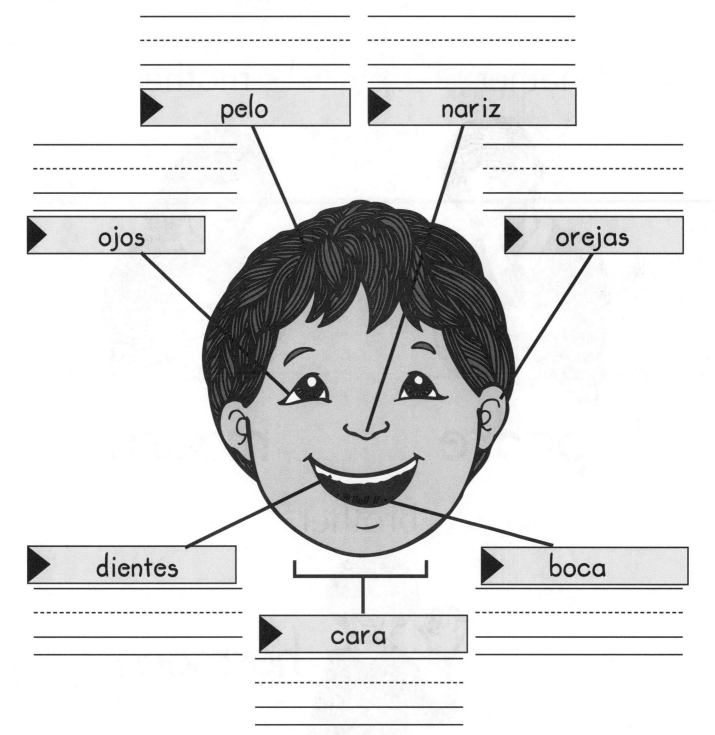

_____   _____
- - - - - - - - - - - - - - - -   - - - - - - - - - - - - - - - -
_____   _____

▶ pelo   ▶ nariz

_____   _____
- - - - - - - - - - - - - - - -   - - - - - - - - - - - - - - - -
_____   _____

▶ ojos   ▶ orejas

▶ dientes   ▶ boca

- - - - - - - - - - - - - - - -   - - - - - - - - - - - - - - - -
_____   _____

▶ cara

- - - - - - - - - - - - - - - -
_____

Which part of your face do you like the best? _____

43   Spanish: Grade 1

Family

Say the family word out loud in English and then in Spanish.

father

padre

mother

madre

brother

hermano

44

Family

Say the family word out loud in English and then in Spanish.

sister

hermana

grandfather

grandmother

abuela

abuelo

Spanish: Grade 1

Family Words

Say each family word out loud.

| madre |  | mother |

| padre |  | father |

| hermana | | sister |

| hermano | | brother |

| abuela |  | grandmother |

| abuelo |  | grandfather |

Name ____________________

My Family

Draw a picture of your family. Color your picture.

Mi familia

Write the correct Spanish word next to each person in your picture above.

padre	hermano	abuelo
madre	hermana	abuela

Community

Say the community word out loud in English and then in Spanish.

biblioteca

library

escuela

park   school

parque

Community

Say the community word out loud in English and then in Spanish.

tienda

grocery store

house

casa

museum

museo

Places to Go

Say the Spanish words out loud.

escuela		school
museo		museum
casa		house
tienda		store
biblioteca		library
parque		park

Our Town

Draw a picture of a town showing the community places named at the bottom of the page. Label the places in Spanish.

escuela	museo	casa
biblioteca	tienda	parque

Classroom Objects

Say the name of the classroom object out loud in English and then in Spanish.

libro

book

pencil

lápiz

scissors

tijeras

52

Classroom Objects

Say the name of the classroom object out loud in English and then in Spanish.

borrador
eraser

chair

table
mesa

silla

Classroom Things

Say each word out loud.

silla		chair
libro		book
mesa		table
lápiz		pencil
tijeras		scissors
borrador		eraser

54

Matching Objects

Draw a line from the word to the correct picture. Color the picture.

silla

libro

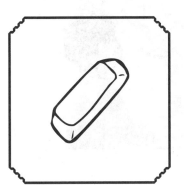

mesa

lápiz

tijeras

borrador

Songs and Chants

¡Hola! Means Hello
(to the tune of "London Bridge")

¡Hola! means hello-o-o, hello-o-o, hello-o-o.
¡Hola! means hello-o-o. ¡Hola, amigos!

¡Adiós! Means Good-bye
(to the tune of "London Bridge")

¡Adiós! means goo-ood-bye, goo-ood-bye, goo-ood-bye.
¡Adiós! means goo-ood-bye. ¡Adiós, amigos!

Cinco amigos
(to the tune of "Ten Little Fingers")

Uno, dos, tres, cuatro, cinco,
Uno, dos, tres, cuatro, cinco,
Uno, dos, tres, cuatro, cinco,
Cinco amigos son.

Songs and Chants

Diez amigos

(to the tune of "Ten Little Fingers")

Uno, dos, tres amigos,
cuatro, cinco, seis amigos,
siete, ocho, nueve amigos,
diez amigos son.

Diez, nueve, ocho amigos,
siete, seis, cinco amigos,
cuatro, tres, dos amigos,
un amigo es.

Colors Song

(to the tune of "Twinke, Twinkle Little Star")

Red is rojo,   green is verde,
purple, morado,   brown, café;
yellow, amarillo,   blue, azul,
pink is rosado,   orange, anaranjado;
white is blanco,   black is negro,
colors, colores,   colors, colores.

Songs and Chants

Classroom Objects Song

(to the tune of "The Farmer in the Dell")

A silla is a chair;
A libro is a book;
A mesa is a table in our classroom.

A lápiz is a pencil;
Tijeras are scissors;
A borrador is an eraser in our classroom.

Clothing Song

(to the tune of "Skip to My Lou")

Camisa — shirt, pantalones — pants,
vestido — dress, calcetines — socks,
zapatos — shoes, gorro — cap
These are the clothes that we wear.

58

Songs and Chants

Family Song
(to the tune of "Are You Sleeping?")

Padre — father,
madre — mother,
chico — boy,
chica — girl,
abuelo is grandpa,
abuela is grandma.
Our family, our family.

Hermano — brother,
hermana — sister,
chico — boy,
chica — girl,
padre y madre,
abuelo y abuela.
Our family, our family.

Clothing Song
(to the tune of "Skip to My Lou")

Camisa — shirt, *pantalones* — pants,
vestido — dress, *calcetines* — socks,
zapatos — shoes, *gorro* — cap.
These are the clothes that we wear.

Chaqueta — jacket, *botas* — boots,
abrigo — dress, *falda* — skirt,
guantes are gloves. What did we forget?
Pantalones cortos are shorts.

Animals Song
(to the tune of "This Old Man")

Gato — cat,
perro — dog,
pájaro is a flying bird,
pez is a fish, and
pato is a duck,
culebra is a slinky snake.

Spanish: Grade 1

Songs and Chants

Community Song
(to the tune of "Here We Go 'Round the Mulberry Bush")

Escuela is school,
museo — museum,
casa is house,
tienda is store,
biblioteca is library,
parque is the park for me!

Alphabet Song
(to the tune of "B-I-N-G-O")

A   B   C   D   E   F   G
(There was   a   farmer had   a   dog)

H   I   J   K
(and Bin-   go   was his   name-o.)

L   M   N   Ñ   O
(B   I   N   G   O)

P   Q   R   S   T
(B   I   N   G   O)

U   V   W
(B   I   N G O)

X   Y   Z
(and   Bingo was his   name-o.)

60

Numbers

Cut out the learning cards. Practice saying the Spanish words using the learning cards.

0 cero

1 uno

2 dos

3 tres

4 cuatro

5 cinco

This page is intentionally left blank.

Numbers and the Face

Cut out the learning cards. Practice saying the Spanish words using the learning cards.

This page is intentionally left blank.

The Face

Cut out the learning cards. Practice saying the Spanish words using the learning cards.

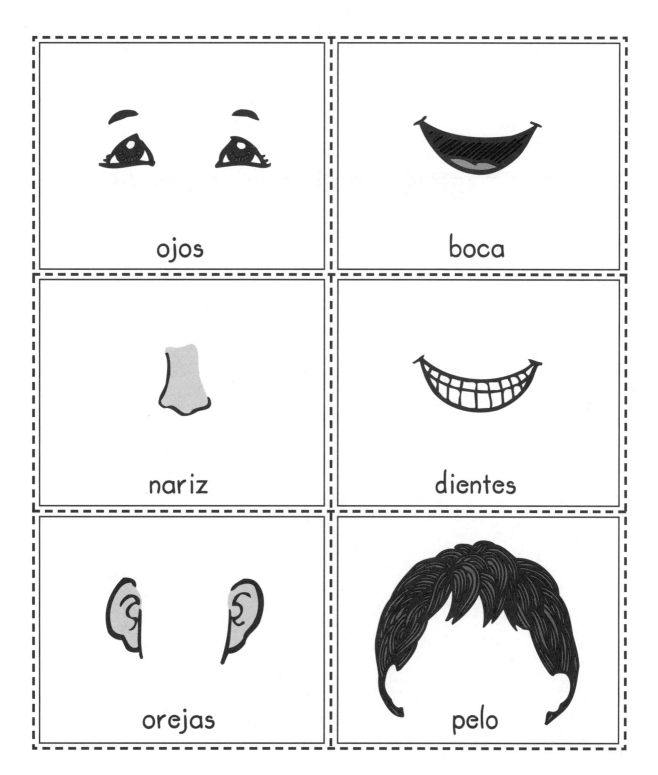

ojos

boca

nariz

dientes

orejas

pelo

Spanish: Grade 1

This page is intentionally left blank.

Colors

Cut out the learning cards. Practice saying the Spanish words using the learning cards.

rojo

azul

verde

anaranjado

morado

amarillo

Spanish: Grade 1

This page is intentionally left blank.

68

Colors and Food

Cut out the learning cards. Practice saying the Spanish words using the learning cards.

café

negro

blanco

rosado

pollo

queso

69

Spanish: Grade 1

This page is intentionally left blank.

Food

Cut out the learning cards. Practice saying the Spanish words using the learning cards.

ensalada

pan

jugo

leche

papa

naranja

Spanish: Grade 1

This page is intentionally left blank.

Food

Cut out the learning cards. Practice saying the Spanish words using the learning cards.

carne

plátano

sopa

agua

sandwich

manzana

73

This page is intentionally left blank.

Family

Cut out the learning cards. Practice saying the Spanish words using the learning cards.

This page is intentionally left blank.

76

Numbers Review

Write the number next to the Spanish word. Circle the correct number of animals for each number shown. Then, color the pictures.

uno | 1
cinco | 5
dos | 2
cuatro | 4
tres | 3

Colors Will Vary.

7

Matching Numbers

Draw a line from the word to the correct picture. Then, color the pictures.

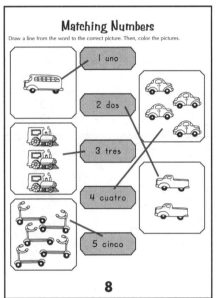

1 uno
2 dos
3 tres
4 cuatro
5 cinco

8

Number the Stars

Draw the correct number of stars next to each number.

uno ★
dos ★ ★
tres ★ ★ ★
cuatro ★ ★ ★ ★
cinco ★ ★ ★ ★ ★

9

1–10 Matching

Draw a line to match each object to the number that is written in Spanish.

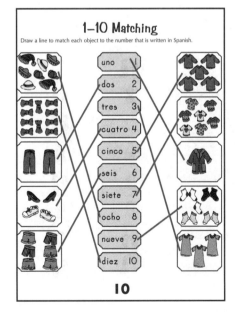

uno 1
dos 2
tres 3
cuatro 4
cinco 5
seis 6
siete 7
ocho 8
nueve 9
diez 10

10

Count the Cookies

In each box at the left, write the number that matches the Spanish word. Cross out the correct number of cookies to show the number written in Spanish. The first one is done for you.

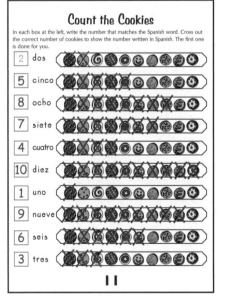

2 dos
5 cinco
8 ocho
7 siete
4 cuatro
10 diez
1 uno
9 nueve
6 seis
3 tres

11

Spanish: Grade 1

My Favorite Number

Write your favorite number from 1 to 10 in the boxes. Draw a picture to show that number.

My favorite number is ☐ .

In Spanish, it is called [Answers Will Vary.] .

[Pictures Will Vary.]

12

Circles 1–10

Draw the correct number of circles in each box.

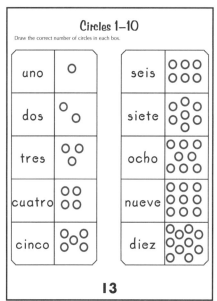

13

Coloring 0–10

Color or circle the number of butterflies that shows the number written in Spanish.

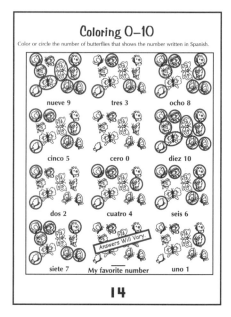

nueve 9   tres 3   ocho 8

cinco 5   cero 0   diez 10

dos 2   cuatro 4   seis 6

[Answers Will Vary.]

siete 7   My favorite number   uno 1

14

Listening Practice

Say the Spanish word for each number out loud.
Write the first letter of the words you hear.

1 u   4 c   7 s

2 d   5 c   8 o

3 t   6 s   9 n

Color the letters of the Spanish alphabet. Say them in Spanish as you color them.

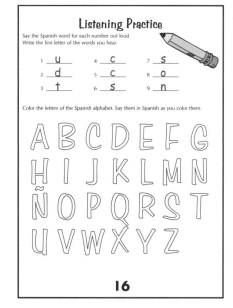

A B C D E F G
H I J K L M N
Ñ O P Q R S T
U V W X Y Z

16

Pictures of Greetings

Say the greeting out loud. Circle the picture that tells the meaning of each word.

¡Hola!

¿Cómo te llamas?

Me llamo…

¿Cómo estás?

bien

mal

así, así

¡Adiós!

22

Seven Days

Copy the Spanish words for the days of the week. In Spanish-speaking countries, *lunes* is the first day of the week.

Monday	lunes	lunes
Tuesday	martes	martes
Wednesday	miércoles	miércoles
Thursday	jueves	jueves
Friday	viernes	viernes
Saturday	sábado	sábado
Sunday	domingo	domingo

Draw a line to match the Spanish and English days of the week.

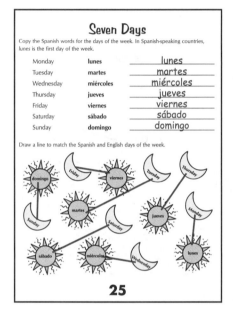

25

Colors Introduction

Say the words out loud. Color the word with the correct color.

28

My Meal

Draw or cut out pictures of food and glue them on the plate to make a meal. Which food is your favorite?

Mi comida

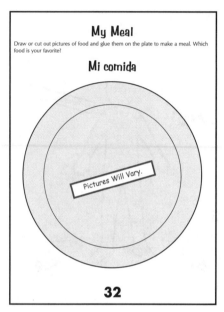

Pictures Will Vary.

32

Animal Crossword

Use the picture clues to complete the puzzle. Choose from the Spanish words at the bottom of the page. One is done for you.

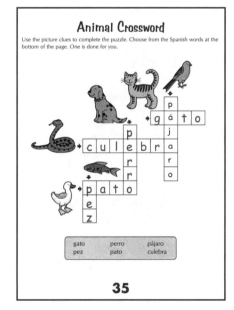

| gato | perro | pájaro |
| pez | pato | culebra |

35

Clothing Match-Ups

Draw a line from the word to the correct picture. Color the picture.

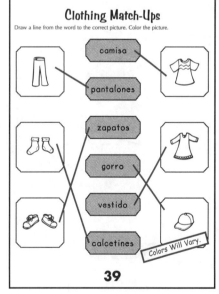

camisa
pantalones
zapatos
gorro
vestido
calcetines

Colors Will Vary.

39

Spanish: Grade 1

How Are You?

Draw or cut out pictures of clothes to make a boy or girl. Write the names of the clothes next to them in Spanish.

Who are you?

Pictures Will Vary.

How are you?

What are you wearing?

40

What's on Your Face?

Say each word out loud. Copy each word.

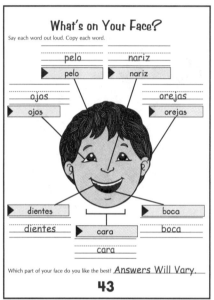

pelo
pelo

nariz
nariz

ojos
ojos

orejas
orejas

dientes

boca

dientes

cara
boca

cara

Which part of your face do you like the best? **Answers Will Vary.**

43

My Family

Draw a picture of your family. Color your picture.

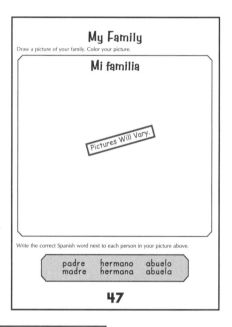

Mi familia

Pictures Will Vary.

Write the correct Spanish word next to each person in your picture above.

padre	hermano	abuelo
madre	hermana	abuela

47

Our Town

Draw a picture of a town showing the community places named at the bottom of the page. Label the places in Spanish.

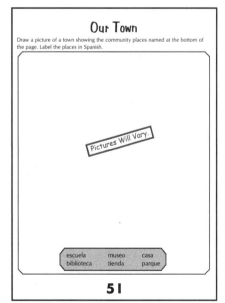

Pictures Will Vary.

escuela	museo	casa
biblioteca	tienda	parque

51

Matching Objects

Draw a line from the word to the correct picture. Color the picture.

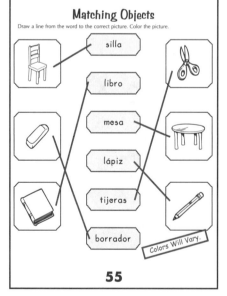

silla

libro

mesa

lápiz

tijeras

borrador

Colors Will Vary.

55